CONTENTS

INTRODUCTION 4

KNOW YOUR GUITAR....................5

STRINGS AND THINGS 8

HOLDING THE GUITAR 9

AMPS AND EFFECTS 10

RIGHT-HAND POSITION....................12

LEFT-HAND POSITION 15

TUNING YOUR GUITAR 16

THE A CHORD 18

THE D CHORD....................20

THE E CHORD....................22

DOWNSTROKES AND UPSTROKES 24

MIDNIGHT SPECIAL....................26

THE C CHORD 27

THE F CHORD....................28

THE G CHORD 29

PLAYING C, F AND G 30

THE A MINOR CHORD 31

HOUSE OF THE RISING SUN 32

BAR CHORDS 33

THE D MINOR CHORD 35

THE G^7 CHORD....................36

FOUR-CHORD PROGRESSION:
    C–AM–DM–G^7 37

THE E MINOR CHORD 38

FOUR-CHORD PROGRESSION:
    G–EM–AM–D 39

THE A^7 CHORD 40

THE B^7 CHORD 41

THE D^7 CHORD....................42

THE E^7 CHORD 43

THE AM^7 CHORD 44

THE DM^7 CHORD....................45

ITSY BITSY TEENIE WEENIE 46

CONGRATULATIONS!....................48

Welcome to *Beginning Guitar.* The guitar remains one of the world's most popular instruments. This book will guide you from the very first time you take your guitar out of its case to playing your first song.

Easy-to-follow instructions will guide you through:

• how to take care of your guitar
• how to tune it
• how hold the guitar
• learning your first chords
• playing your first songs

Watch the DVD when you need help. The video instruction will show you how to properly place your fingers on the fretboard and will allow you to hear what you should be playing. The video lessons are referenced by this symbol .

Practice regularly and often. Twenty minutes every day is far better than two hours on the weekend with nothing in between. Not only are you training your brain to understand how to play the guitar, you are also teaching your muscles to memorize certain repeated actions.

Beginning Guitar

Let Amanda and Melissa show you the way!

Packed with full-color photos & diagrams, plus a great DVD.

Learning was never this much fun!

Tomcat Books
A PART OF THE MUSIC SALES GROUP
New York/London/Paris/Sydney/Copenhagen/
Berlin/Tokyo/Madrid

Project editor: David Bradley
Photography: Martin LePire
Models: Melissa Freed, Amanda Evans, and Noelle Joye.
Cover design: Len Vogler
Interior design and layout: Len Vogler

Order No. AM 996820
ISBN: 978-0-8256-3710-0

Exclusive Distributors:
Music Sales Corporation
257 Park Avenue South, New York, NY 10010 USA
Music Sales Limited
14-15 Berners Street, London W1T 3LJ England
Music Sales Pty. Limited
20 Resolution Drive, Caringbah, NSW 2229, Australia

Printed in China

Electric

Acoustic

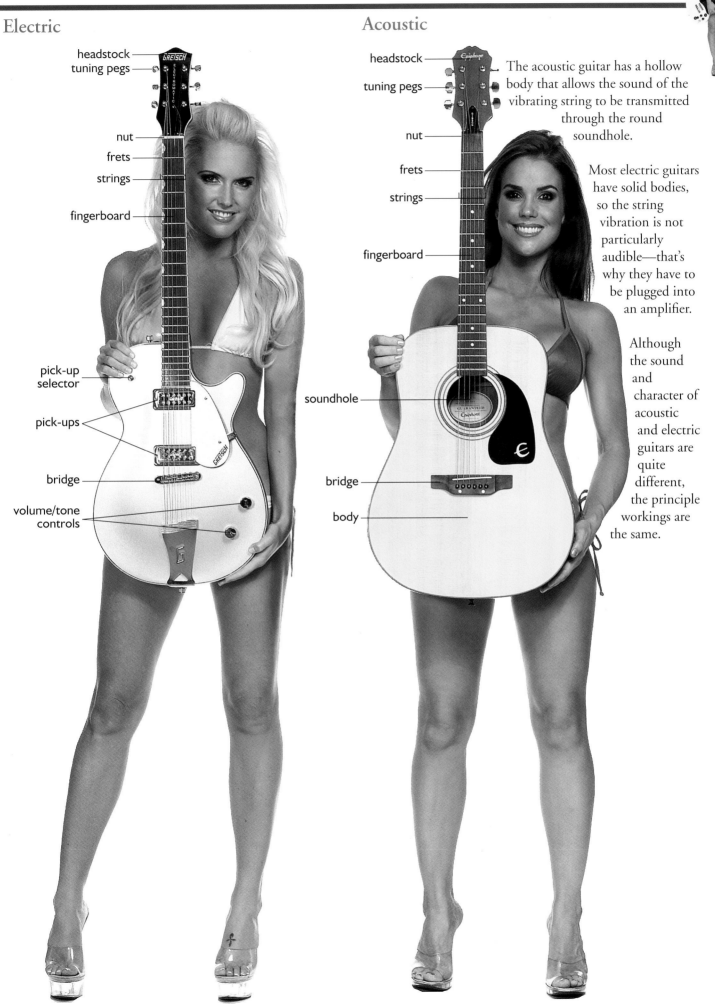

headstock
tuning pegs

nut
frets
strings

fingerboard

pick-up
selector

pick-ups

bridge

volume/tone
controls

headstock

tuning pegs

nut

frets

strings

fingerboard

soundhole

bridge

body

The acoustic guitar has a hollow body that allows the sound of the vibrating string to be transmitted through the round soundhole.

Most electric guitars have solid bodies, so the string vibration is not particularly audible—that's why they have to be plugged into an amplifier.

Although the sound and character of acoustic and electric guitars are quite different, the principle workings are the same.

The headstock (at the end of the fretboard) has six tuning pegs, either three each side or all six in a row.

The strings traverse the fretboard (usually rosewood or maple), which may have plastic or tortoiseshell inlays to help you see where you are on the neck. They are called *position markers.*

position markers

There are dots on the side of the neck at given fret positions as well. Markers are usually placed at frets 3, 5, 7, 9 and 12. Sometimes there are two markers at the twelfth fret.

fret markers

The tuning pegs, or machine heads, consist of a metal capstan and a cog to tension the string.

The strings are kept in place by the nut as they leave the headstock.

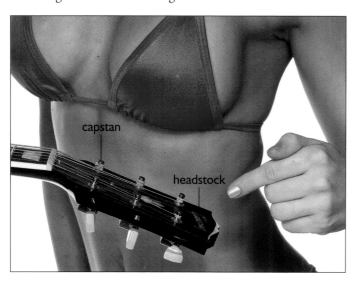

capstan

headstock

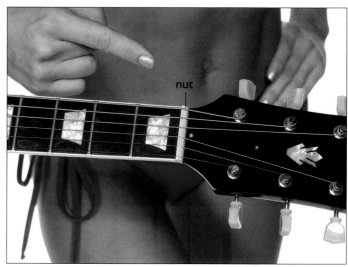

nut

The strings are attached to the body at the bridge, which comes in all shapes and sizes depending on the guitar, but in all cases acts to alter the harmonics and string height.

The bridge on an acoustic guitar is normally fixed and is therefore not adjustable, but on electrics a wide range of string adjustments can usually be made.

Below the strings and bridge, most electric guitars have controls for volume and tone.

The pick-up selector on the Les Paul type guitar is positioned above the strings; on the Fender Stratocaster type it is positioned below the bridge.

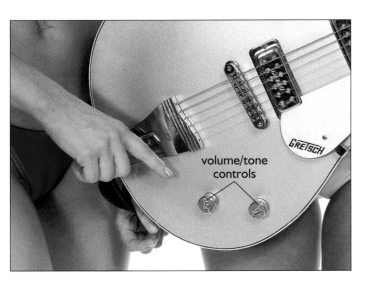

Most electric guitars come with a strap attachment.

Tip

When not being played, try to keep your guitar in its case, away from heat and direct sunlight, where it can't be knocked over. Avoid exposing the instrument to extremes of temperature.

There is nothing quite like the tone of new strings on your guitar, but that sound will soon fade. Strings are made from alloy and tarnish easily, thus losing tone. To extend their life, always wipe down the instrument at the end of each playing session. A clean, dry linen or silk cloth wiped over the strings will remove dirt and moisture.

Strings vary in thickness from the bottom (thickest) to the top (thinnest). The bottom three are wound to give the sound more depth; the top three are just unwound alloy wire. When it's time to change your strings always check that you have the right gauges.

The diameter of a string—its *gauge*—is measured in inches or centimeters: the lower the number, the thinner the string. A set of light gauge strings (0.09–0.42) may be preferable for electric guitar because it makes string-bending easier. An acoustic guitar uses steel strings and can range from light (0.10–0.47) to heavy (0.13–0.57), depending on the style of music you like to play. You might like a lighter string if you are finger-picker (although there are finger-style players that like a heavier string) or a heavier string if you like blues or slide playing.

Once you have decided on the kind of music you like and after you have been playing for a while, you will settle on a string gauge that is right for you. Most players change their minds about strings over the course of their playing career.

There is a new breed of string that is "dipped" in a coating of plastic. This increases the life of the string. The coating stops corrosion that occurs on regular steel strings.

A classical guitar is built to use nylon strings, which place much less tension on the neck than steel strings. In other words, never try to put steel strings on a classical guitar.

Following some simple guidelines will ensure that you always feel comfortable when playing:

1. Your arms should never take the weight of the guitar; they should be free just to play it.

2. Always keep the neck pointing slightly above the horizontal. Never let it point down toward the ground.

3. When practicing, it's more comfortable to sit down. Some players cross their legs right over left and rest the guitar on the right thigh, which elevates the instrument slightly.

4. If you stand, you should not be supporting the guitar. Adjust the strap so the guitar is at a sensible height and position it so there is an equal balance of weight. When you take your hands away it should sit comfortably.

If you have an electric guitar, you'll also need an amplifier and a guitar cable to get a sound out of your instrument. Here's a step-by-step guide to setting up:

1. Attach your guitar strap. Make sure that the strap is adjusted to a comfortable length. A low-slung guitar looks really cool but is actually much more difficult to play. As long as your right and left hands feel comfortable on the guitar your position is probably right.

2. Plug one end of your guitar cable into the guitar. On a Les Paul type guitar (as shown here) the socket is on the underside of the body of the guitar. On a Fender Stratocaster type you will find the socket on the front of the guitar under the tone controls.

3. Take the other end of the cable and plug it into the socket marked "input" on your amplifier.

4. Adjust the volume controls on the amplifier and on your guitar until you can hear a sound from the amplifier.

If you can't hear any sound, check that the amp is plugged in and switched on, and that the volume control on your guitar is turned up.

Now you're ready to play!

If you're lucky enough to have an effects unit such as a distortion or wah-wah pedal, you can have even more fun!

Effects pedals take the sound from your guitar and change it before it gets passed on to the amplifier. They can be powered by batteries or by a separate AC adaptor.

Take another cable and insert one end into the pedal socket marked "output" (or "amplifier") and the other end into the input socket on your amplifier.

Take the other end of the cable that is plugged into your guitar and insert it into the input socket on the pedal (sometimes marked "instrument").

The pedal is activated by simply stomping on the foot-operated switch. When the pedal is not switched on you should still be able hear the sound of your guitar as before. When you step on the switch the sound should change as the effect kicks in.

A wah-wah pedal produces a classic effect that you'll recognize instantly. You plug it in the same way as other effects pedals, and then vary the tone of your guitar sound by rocking back and forth on the pedal.

Once you're happy with your guitar set-up, turn up the volume and make some noise!

Your right hand can strum chords or pick single notes. The best way to start is to strum the strings. Either use a thin (bendy) pick or hold your thumb and first finger together as though you had an imaginary pick. Rest your forearm on the guitar so it can swing freely. Get used to the feel of your strumming hand against the strings.

As an exercise, just strum the strings downward from the 6th string (lowest in pitch) to the 1st.

Then strum down again but go from the 4th to the 1st, skipping over the 5th and 6th strings.

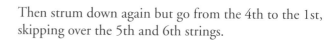

The pick is held between the thumb and index finger of your strumming hand, which should be (roughly) at right angles to each other. Try out a few sizes and thicknesses to find one you're comfortable with. Hold the pick securely and don't have too much of it protruding from your fingers toward the strings.

Now try strumming across the open strings with the pick. Don't worry about your left hand at this stage, just get used to the sensation of the pick traveling across the strings. At first the pick may seem awkward, but this feeling will fade, and it will become an extension of your hand.

Play the open strings one at a time from the 6th to the 1st, then from the 5th to the 1st, 4th to the 1st and so on. Your pick should be hitting the upper side of each string and traveling toward the floor. This is known as a *downstroke*.

Tip

Playing live can be a nerve-racking experience—it's very easy to drop your pick in the heat and sweat of a rock gig. Pro players stick spare picks to the back of their guitar, or wedge them under the pickguard in case of emergencies!

14 • RIGHT-HAND POSITION

Once you're happy with the strumming motion, you can try finger-picking individual strings. The right hand adopts the following position:

1. Rest your forearm lightly on the guitar.

2. Arch your wrist so your fingers are approximately at 60 degrees to the back of your hand, then relax them so they become slightly curved.

3. Place your thumb (p) on the 6th string, your index finger (i) on the 3rd string, your middle finger (m) on the 2nd string and your ring finger (a) on the 1st string. Try to make sure that your thumb comes in contact with the strings about an inch or so in front of your index finger.

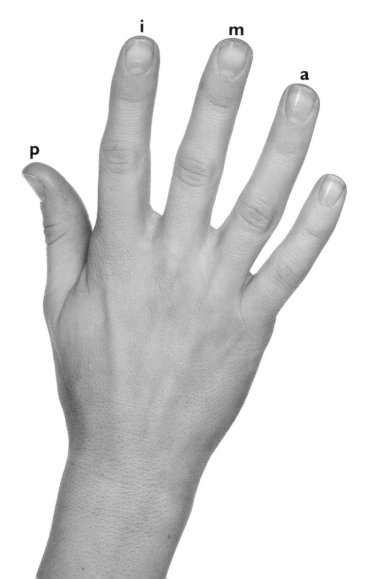

The fretting fingers are numbered 1, 2, 3 and 4.

Try to keep the left hand relaxed. The left-hand thumb should be roughly in the center of the neck behind the first and second fingers.

Tip

The first few weeks will be tough on your fingers. But don't worry! Gradually you'll develop pads of harder skin on the ends of each finger. You'll need to keep practicing to make sure they don't disappear!

The first time you try a new chord you may find it hard to get the positioning of your fingers right, let alone press them down. If necessary, use your other hand to physically put each fretting finger in position.

Once you feel confident holding your guitar, experiment with different playing positions to see what feels the most comfortable. Almost every conceivable playing position has been used at some point—although some are more difficult than others!

CHECKPOINT

WHAT YOU'VE ACHIEVED SO FAR...

You can now:
• Hold your guitar comfortably
• Name each part of the guitar
• Strum with fingers or with a pick
• Choose appropriate strings for your guitar

16•TUNING YOUR GUITAR

There are various ways of tuning the guitar—use the one that suits you best.

Tuning to Another Instrument
The simplest way to make sure that your guitar is in tune is to find someone else with a tuned guitar and match each string on your guitar with the relevant string on the tuned guitar.

Alternatively, you could tune to a piano or electronic keyboard. Refer to the diagram below to tune each string.

6th string E   12th white note below middle C

ⓒ = middle C

5th string A   9th white note below middle C

4th string D   6th white note below middle C

3rd string G   3rd white note below middle C

2nd string B   1st white note below middle C

1st string E   2nd white note above middle C

Tip

If you're playing with other people it's vital that you all tune to the same note. If one of the instruments can't be easily tuned (like a piano for example), make sure that you tune to that.

Electronic Tuners
The best way to tune your guitar is by using an electronic tuner. You can get a basic electronic tuner for under $20. Most electronic tuners come with a built-in microphone, making it possible to tune your acoustic guitar as well.

Tip

If you're not sure whether a note is sharp or flat (i.e., too high or too low), loosen the string being tuned a little and slowly bring it up to the required pitch.

Relative Tuning

This is perhaps the most common method and one that works if you are pretty confident that at least one of the strings is in tune. Let's assume the bottom string (6th) is in tune. Being the thickest, you'll find that the 6th string probably won't drift out of tune as much as some of the others.

Follow the tuning diagram below and tune from the bottom string up to the top string.

To tune:

6th to 5th string	5th to 4th string	4th to 3rd string	3rd to 2nd string	2nd to 1st string

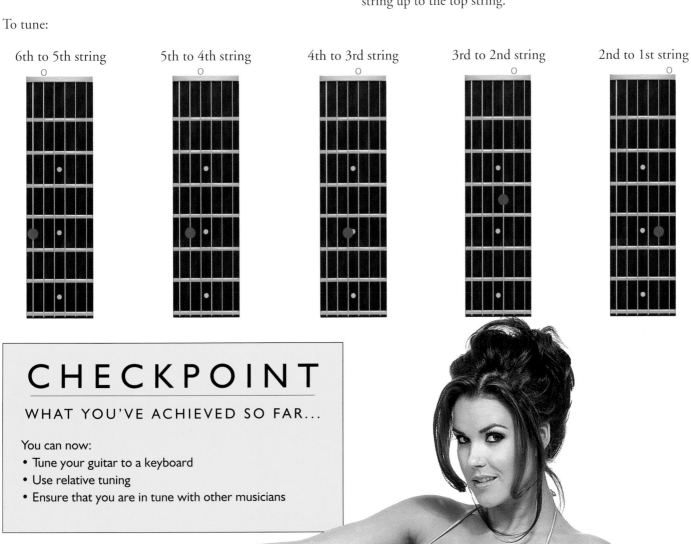

CHECKPOINT

WHAT YOU'VE ACHIEVED SO FAR...

You can now:
- Tune your guitar to a keyboard
- Use relative tuning
- Ensure that you are in tune with other musicians

Now that you've tuned up, let's play some chords. Besides learning the chord fingering, we're going to look at some simple strumming and work all the ideas into a song.

Compare how the A chord looks in the photo to the chord box:

Chords for the guitar are pictured in the form of a "chord box," where the six strings are viewed as though you're looking at the guitar neck with the headstock pointing up and the strings going down. The numbers in circles tell you which fingers to use.

A

Tip

If you're left-handed these numbers will stay the same, but the chord shape itself will be reversed.

x = don't play this string
o = open string
o = open string (root)

1. The fingers are placed just behind the 2nd fret. You never press down a string with a finger actually on the metal fret.

2. The fingers are angled to fit comfortably alongside each other and to fit in the narrow space.

3. The 6th string is not played; the 5th and 1st strings are "open" (i.e., not fretted and shown as 0 in the chord box).

4. Keep the little finger out of the way so it doesn't catch the 1st string.

Now strum the whole chord—just downward strums at first.

Chords and Progressions demonstrates how the A chord should sound.

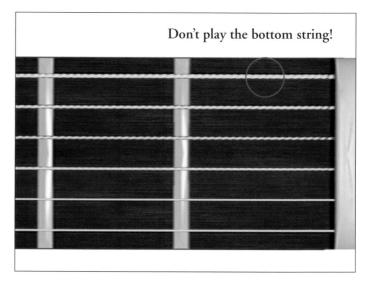

Don't play the bottom string!

A major facts:

1. The A chord's full name is A major—later on you'll come across other types of A chords such as minor and seventh.

2. The A chord is named after its lowest note—the open A string (the 5th string).

3. Like all major chords, A major is characterized by a bright, happy sound.

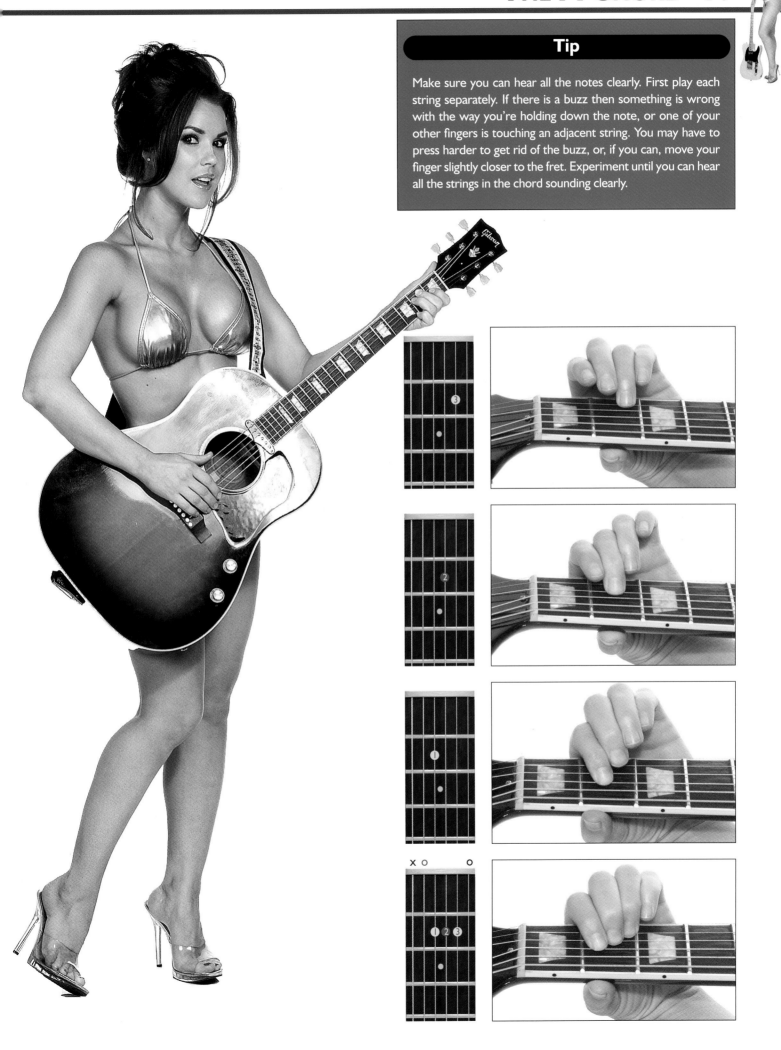

Tip

Make sure you can hear all the notes clearly. First play each string separately. If there is a buzz then something is wrong with the way you're holding down the note, or one of your other fingers is touching an adjacent string. You may have to press harder to get rid of the buzz, or, if you can, move your finger slightly closer to the fret. Experiment until you can hear all the strings in the chord sounding clearly.

Let's try the D chord next. It only has four notes, so don't play the E and A (6th and 5th) strings.

1. The 3rd finger must avoid touching the E string (1st string) for all the strings to sound clearly.

2. Keep your little finger out of the way.

3. Play the strings separately from bottom to top (4th to 1st) and make sure they are all sounding clearly.

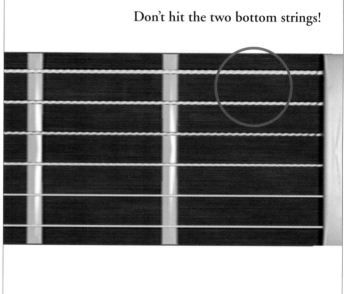

Don't hit the two bottom strings!

4. Now strum the whole chord.

Chords and Progressions demonstrates how the D chord should sound.

D major facts:

1. The D chord is named after its lowest note—the open D string (the 4th string).

2. D is a favorite with folk guitarists. Try adding your 4th finger at the 3rd fret on the top string to form a Dsus4 chord for a classic folk sound.

3. D and A sound great when played after each other.

Don't press down too hard with the fingers of your left hand—you'll be surprised how little pressure it actually takes to fret a chord successfully. Positioning your thumb comfortably behind the neck can be helpful.

You have now learned two of the most common chords in rock—A and D. These two chords sound great when played one after the other. You'll find this chord change in hundreds of classic songs.

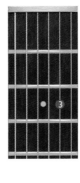 

 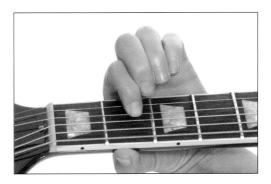

This chord has inspired many classic riffs and songs, and sounds great because you can play all six strings. There are just three strings to fret (5th, 4th, and 3rd):

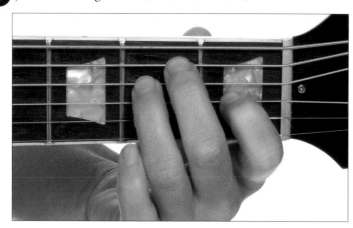

E

E is a powerful sounding chord because all six strings are played, including three open strings that ring out.

Chords and Progressions demonstrates how the E chord should sound.

Although the E chord is a relatively simple shape, be careful not to catch your third finger on the 3rd string—this will stop the note ringing. Your fingertips should adopt more of a vertical position above the strings to avoid this. Relax the thumb and arch the wrist for the best position.

E major facts:

1. The E chord is the fullest sounding of all the chords you've learned so far—because, unlike A or D, it uses all six strings.

2. E is possibly the most popular key for guitar music, because it allows you to use the open E strings (top and bottom strings).

3. Once you've perfected the E shape, try adding your little finger at the 2nd fret, 3rd string, to form an Esus4 chord.

A, D, & E—the three-chord trick

The chords of A, D, and E can be played in almost any sequence and they will always sound good.

In fact, lots of classic rock songs can be played using only these three chords—check out "Wild Thing," "Peggy Sue," or just about any blues tune to hear the three-chord trick in action.

CHECKPOINT

WHAT YOU'VE ACHIEVED SO FAR...

You can now:
- Play the chords of A, D, and E major
- Strum 4-, 5-, or 6-string chords

Now that you're familiar with the chord shapes of A, D, and E, let's do some playing! All you need to concentrate on is counting four beats per measure, as indicated below the staff.

Play this progression with downstrokes only. Chord symbols are shown at each new chord change.

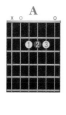     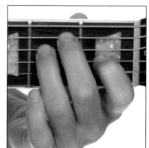

Chords and Progressions demonstrate how the A, D, and E chords sound in a progression.

Downstroke

The ⊓ means that you should strum each chord with a "downstroke," moving from the strings nearest the ceiling down toward the floor (from low to high).

Upstroke

The ∨ means that you should strum each chord with an "upstroke," moving from the strings nearest the floor up toward the ceiling (from high to low).

Now try playing the same progression using downstrokes and upstrokes. Count out loud, "1 & 2 & 3 & 4 &." The downstrokes are played on the numbered beats and the upstrokes are played on the "&"s.

Chords and Progressions demonstrates downstrokes and upstrokes.

26 • MIDNIGHT SPECIAL

So far you have learned three chords. Let's put them to use playing a song. This song is an old tune called *Midnight Special*.

Notice the "down, down-up" strumming pattern. You count it like this: "1 2& 3 4&." Sometimes this pattern is referred to as the "boom–chick-a, boom–chick-a" pattern because of the way it sounds.

MIDNIGHT SPECIAL

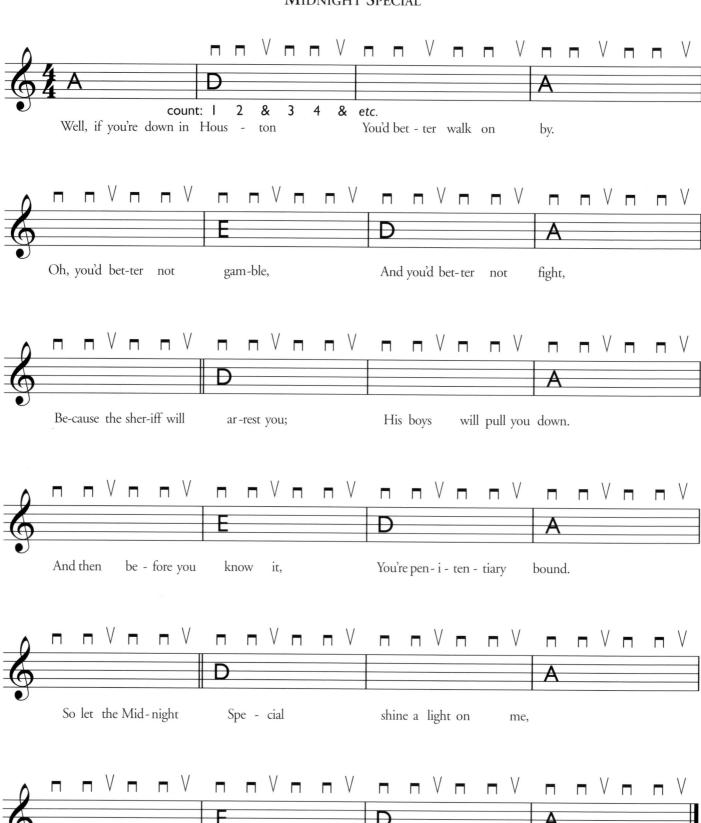

count: 1 2 & 3 4 & *etc.*

Well, if you're down in Hous - ton   You'd bet - ter walk on   by.

Oh, you'd bet-ter not   gam-ble,   And you'd bet-ter not   fight,

Be-cause the sher-iff will   ar-rest you;   His boys   will pull you down.

And then   be - fore you   know   it,   You're pen - i - ten - tiary   bound.

So let the Mid-night   Spe - cial   shine a light on   me,

Oh, let the Mid-night   Spe - cial   shine its ev-er-lov - in' light on   me.

The C chord is a little more difficult than the others you have learned because of the open string in the middle of the chord.

C

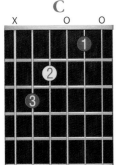

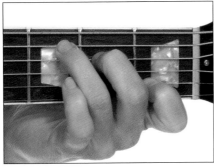

The first finger has to be almost vertical to clear the 1st string, so make sure your nails are short enough to press down onto the 2nd string in this way. Watch out that you don't catch your second finger against the open 3rd string (G). Try to make your fingertips meet the fingerboard at right angles.

Chords and Progressions demonstrates how to play the C chord.

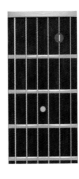

The F chord is a lot like the C chord, but this chord requires you to use your first finger to press down both the 1st and 2nd strings at the 1st fret (called a *bar*). This is hard at first, but with a little practice it will become easier. Playing the F chord as shown is sometimes called the "baby" F chord. Later you will be introduced to the full-bar F, which is a fuller sounding F chord because it uses all six strings.

Again, like the C chord, try to keep your second and third fingers at right angles.

Chords and Progressions demonstrates how to play the F chord.

 = bar.

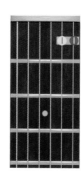

The last chord in this series in the G chord. Make sure when you play the G chord that you arch your fingers to avoid muting the open strings.

You will have to practice going from the C or F to the G. It will take a while to get your fingers used to moving between the various chord shapes, but it will come with practice.

Chords and Progressions demonstrates how to play the G chord.

Using the new chords you've learned, let's play a new progression: C–F–G.

Chords and Progressions demonstrates how to play the C–F–G progression.

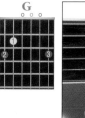

The next progression uses a new strumming pattern. This is a "down, down, down-up, down-up" pattern and is counted like this: "1 2 3& 4&."

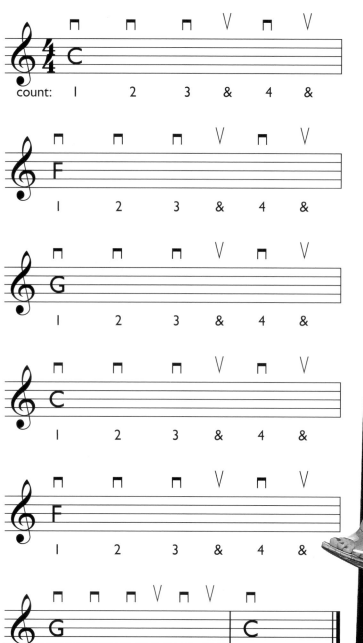

Up until now you have only learned major chords. Let's increase your chord library by adding some minor chords. The next chord you will learn is A minor. The A minor chord (Am) is used in many rock and folk tunes.

Even though the A minor and A major sound much different from each other, notice that there is only one note changed and by one fret.

Four-Chord Progressions demonstrates how to play the Am chord.

Am

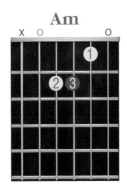

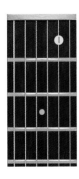

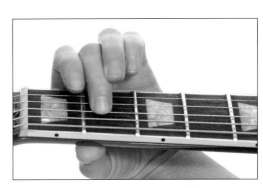

32 • HOUSE OF THE RISING SUN

Now that you have the Am chord in your arsenal, let's try another song. This is an old classic called *House of the Rising Sun.*

The song is in ⅝ time. This means there are six beats to a measure. It's counted like this: "1 2 3& 4 5 6."

HOUSE OF THE RISING SUN

intro

| **Am** | **C** | **D** | **F** |

count: 1 2 3 & 4 5 6 etc.

| **Am** | **E** | **Am** | **E** |

There

verse

| **Am** | **C** | **D** | **F** |

is   a house   in New   Or - leans   they

| **Am** | **G** | **E** | **E** |

call   the Ris -   ing Sun.   It's

| **Am** | **C** | **D** | **F** |

been   the ruin   of many   a poor boy   and

| **Am** | **E** | **Am** | **E** |

God,   I know   I'm one.

The *bar chord* is an essential part of playing the guitar. Let's start with the full F major bar chord. Place your first finger across all six strings at the 1st fret. Then put your second finger on the 2nd fret of the 3rd string, your third finger on the 3rd fret of the 5th string, and your fourth finger on the 3rd fret of the 4th string. This takes a while to get use to, but with practice and persistance it will become fairly natural.

Bar Chords demonstrates how to play the F major bar chord.

F

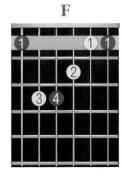

34 • BAR CHORDS

Now that you know how to play a major bar chord, you are able to play every major chord because this shape is movable. The example below shows the F, G, A, and B chords.

Bar Chords demonstrates how to play the F, G, A, and B bar chords.

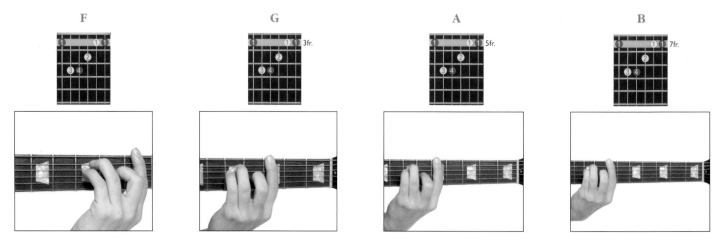

The chart below shows all the major chords up the neck to the 12th fret and back down the neck to the 1st fret. When going up the neck chords are sharped (like A to A♯), but when going down the neck chords are flatted (like B to B♭). Play these chords using downstrokes.

More About Bar Chords demonstrates how to play all the following bar chords.

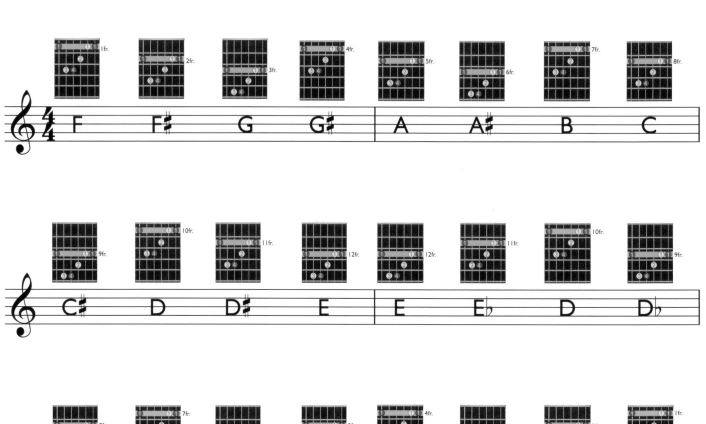

The next new minor chord is D minor.

Four-Chord Progressions demonstrates how to play the Dm chord.

Dm

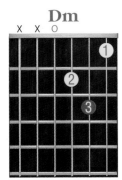

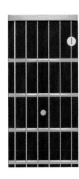

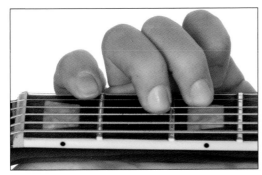

The last chord you will learn before playing your first four-chord progression is a G^7.

Four-Chord Progressions demonstrates how to play the G^7 chord.

Let's combine our new chords (Am, Dm, and G⁷) with the C chord to create a new four-chord progression.

Four-Chord Progressions demonstrates how to play this new progression.

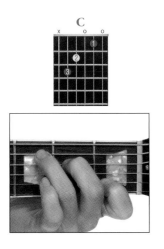
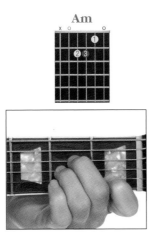
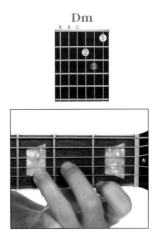
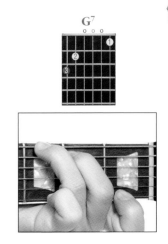

Play the C–Am–Dm–G⁷ progression using downstrokes and upstrokes.

38 • THE E MINOR CHORD

The last progression that you are going to play uses an E minor chord. Just form an E major shape and lift off your first finger.

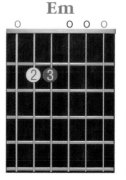

Em

Alternate Fingerings

The fingerings used in this book are the most common and easiest to play. However, they are merely suggestions. You will find that using alternate fingerings may make certain chord changes flow more smoothly.

Four-Chord Progressions demonstrates how to play the Em chord.

FOUR-CHORD PROGRESSION: G–EM–AM–D • 39

For our final progression we will use the Em chord along with the Am, G, and D chords that we learned earlier.

Four-Chord Progressions demonstrates how to play this progression.

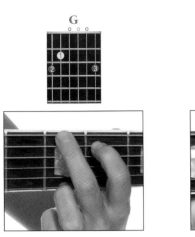
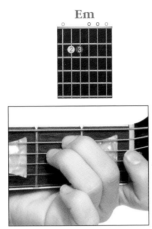
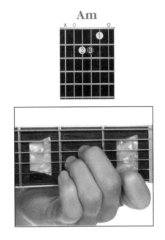
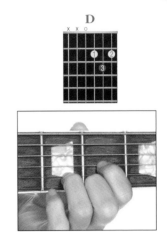

Play this progression using up- and downstrokes.

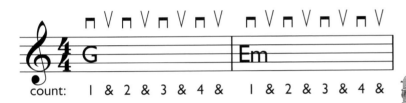

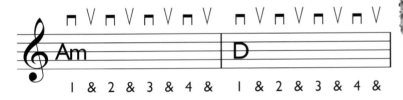

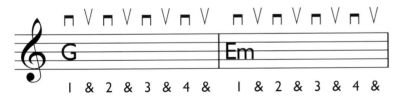

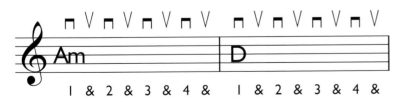

These last few pages will provide you with some very useful chords. The A⁷ is just like the A chord—you just lift up your second finger to leave the 3rd string open.

A⁷

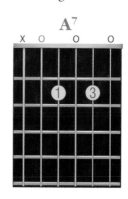
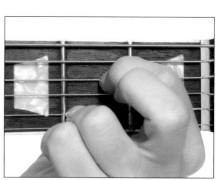

The B⁷ chord can be difficult at first. Make sure the open 2nd string rings out clearly.

B⁷

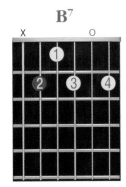 

D⁷ looks like an inverted D chord.

D⁷

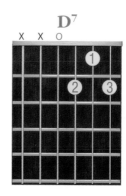

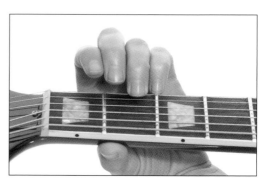

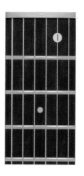

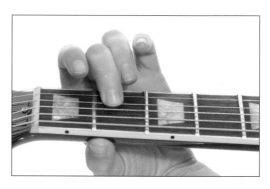

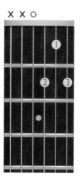

Make an E chord and lift up your third finger—you've just made an E⁷ chord, another guitar favorite.

E⁷

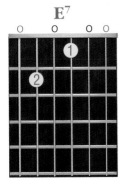

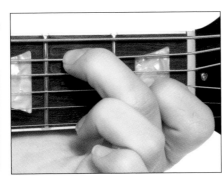

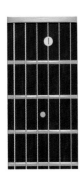

44 • THE AM⁷ CHORD

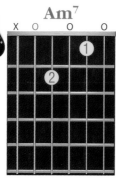

Am⁷

A minor 7 (Am⁷) looks just like E⁷—move your first and second fingers over to the 4th and 2nd strings. Try changing between Am⁷ and E⁷ for an instant two-chord song.

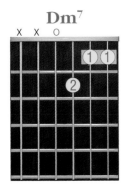

Dm⁷

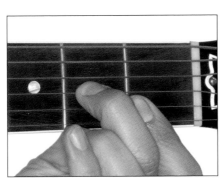

The Dm⁷ has a subtle jazz feel. Notice that the top three strings form the baby F chord we learned earlier.

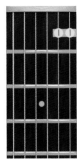

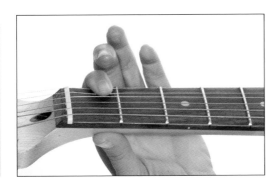

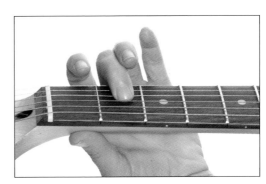

46 • Itsy Bitsy Teenie Weenie

You've made it to the end and now it's time for our last song:

Itsy Bitsy Teenie Weenie Yellow Polka Dot Bikini

Words and Music by Paul Vance and Lee Pockriss

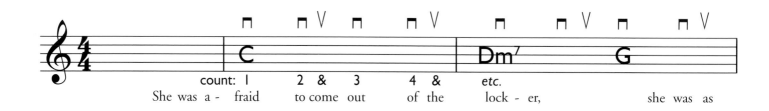

count: 1   2 & 3   4 &   etc.

She was a-fraid   to come out   of the   lock-er,   she was as

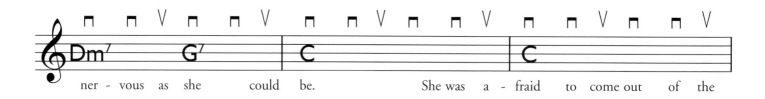

ner-vous as she   could be.   She was a-fraid   to come out   of the

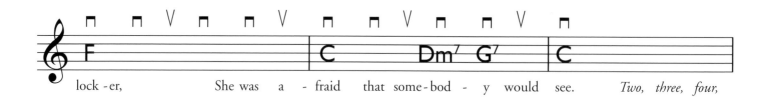

lock-er,   She was a-fraid   that some-bod-y would see.   *Two, three, four,*

chorus

count: 1   &   2   &   3   &   4   & etc.

tell the people what she wore.   It   was   an   it-sy   bit-sy   tee-nie   wee-nie

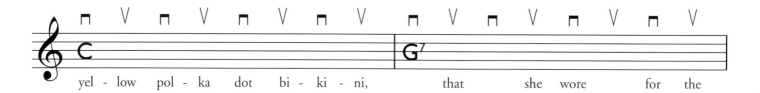

yel-low pol-ka dot bi-ki-ni,   that   she   wore   for the

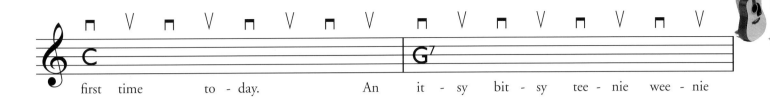

first time   to - day.   An   it - sy   bit - sy   tee - nie   wee - nie

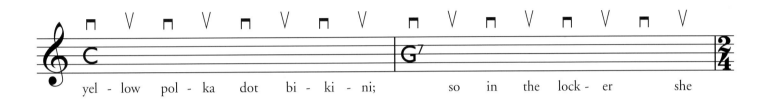

yel - low   pol - ka   dot   bi - ki - ni;   so   in   the   lock - er   she

count: 1   &   2   &
want - ed   to   stay.

We hope that you have enjoyed playing through *Beginning Guitar* and that you will feel inspired to continue making music on your guitar in whichever style most interests you. Feel free to ask other players about their experience and techniques—they'll be able to pass on some useful tips and advice.

If you've made it this far, you've learned many guitar chords and, more importantly, you have learned to change between them smoothly. You've learned to strum in various patterns using both upstrokes and downstrokes, and you've developed your sense of rhythm. Finally, you've put all those skills together and learned a few songs.

Keep playing and good luck!